T0159002

SHORT VERSE GOES TRENDY

ANNETTE STOVALL

authorHOUSE®

AuthorHouse™
1663 Liberty Drive
Bloomington, IN 47403
www.authorhouse.com
Phone: 1 (800) 839-8640

Published by AuthorHouse 11/20/2018

ISBN: 978-1-5462-5976-3 (sc)
ISBN: 978-1-5462-5975-6 (e)

Library of Congress Control Number: 2018910855

Print information available on the last page.

This book is printed on acid-free paper.

Contents

Trends of Today 1

Some Apparel Trends Today 2

A Living Custom 3

With Things Invented 4

Expressive Along Trend 5

It's a Style Medium Too Much 6

Too Large, Too Small 7

Decade Questions with Trendy or Not 8

Designing Buy or Not 9

Buying This or That 10

Trend With Food 11

Then to Home I Come 12

Observation 13

To President Promises 15

I Cherish Love 16

Customary Supermarket 17

Another Day with Supermarket 18

Enters Mr. Pounds 19

Her Custom Dark Hours She in Residence 20

A Customary Time Life Generated 21

Two for the Wealth 22

This Age Revolving Trend 23

They Special This Way 24

Tighten Up 25

Inventions Etcetera 26

This Little Poem I Love 27

There Is No Doubt The Poet's Show 28

Profiling Trends With How She Is 29

Custom Beside The True Guides 30

Another Trend Tomorrow 31

A Day With Perception 32

Let Truth Be Told 33

In This World We Live 34

Name Calling 35

My Design is to Be 36

Incident Assessed to Bar Habit 37

Customarily Before He goes to Sleep 38

Habits Paradigms Between 39

Nocturnal Jamboree Custom 40

Loves a Grandmother Missing 41

Refers to Habit Neighbor Loved 42

Which Route to Travel 43

Union Entitles Trend 44

Expressive of a Tippler 45

Symmetry Styles 46

Designs on Adam and Eve 47

Fight The Unrelenting Trap 48

Overseen at Farmstead 49

Cecil 50

Liquid Sounds 51

Good Looks, Age Regardless 52

Mature About Profile 53

Sage and Witty Comments 54

In Close 56

Trend in Competition 57

Awareness Along The Route 58

Centenarians About Friendship 59

How Soon They Fly 60

Be Warned Of Lateness Calls 61

Arouse the Sleep Alive to Western Custom 62

Gone One Little Lad's Love 63

Concerning Stranger 64

Employing Maxim 65

Responsive of a Female 66

Trend As In Contemporary 67

Empty Designs.. 68
A Word About Who Smokes.. 69
Directive 70
Vestige from the Graves.. 71
What Achieving Glory Meant.. 72

Of Trends, Customs, Designs And Odds

Trends of Today

Things are looking better the more
from what designs decades ago.
Instead of thick bulky old fashioned Tv frames,
today, it's flat screen Cable Tv faming
color tints picture instead of black and white the same.

Instead of plain square telephone jet black and big,
today, the wireless manifold tints wee Cell Phone legit.
The inches bit iPhone trendy, for if your question exact,
on the screen, it answers it right away back.
Computer jet ink print sends the page e-mail
instead of you post your own ebony ink written mail.
Electric Clothes Washer, Dryer, Juicer, stay trendy steady
with DVD Player, Dish Washer, lighter weight and Robot grade
floor Vacuums better made.

Microwave Oven, fast cooking Pots, Electric Grills in style
as also the Super Jet Liner, Electric and Hybrid Cars
and wireless machines the in-thing style.
Designs today, help us do what desired.
And these all just a few admired.

Some Apparel Trends Today

I stopped at apparel clothes mart one day,
and, Oh, what did I see to say.
Tights, mini-skirts, leggings
since many women, today, don't buy dresses.
Tall boots, wide brim hats making comeback
beside African design turbans, Chinese style brim caps
youngsters wear as do men and women.
Fiery rust shirt, loud yellow amber goldlike tunic
looked attractive to virtually anyone there too.
I left wearing mini-patchwork in across strap body bag purse
and faux fur top deep tan boots
and just in time to see sneakers bright purple streak shoes
a child wearing that won't mod fashion of inhibit new
styles men and women sneakers, also, now.
Suddenly, my eyebrows piqued how looking "Wow,"
at fossil brown and black cast leopard blots
fashioned odd the blotch spot tones a car wearing.
Today, I say with little and no regret,
Heavens, what will they think of next!

A Living Custom

Should I to bare a custom in earth's crust
Scored if on land or trail or distant shore,
How free to earth this notable custom!
Because all turf designed in what furthermore.
Need I to bare turf crossing loam too far
And after point where lilies ray the hill?
No, here, I bare how group alliance star.
Such spirit, such drive dents what bridges ill!
I know such drive like drive the blacks own
With whom also the rate in group makes claim
Of shame and tribulation we all moan!
Know, too, if nothing comes bridging less pain.

And after all that else I have known,
I find myself with triumph I have known.

With Things Invented

We sit inside the soft seat for chair
And think about how warm it is out where
Out is adjusting solar system so hot
It sweats debris on the rock orbs sun pecked lot.
We feel we are safe because a means plan became made
Endows us air we sit calm in the shade
Of a fan or sit for ardent summer's chill room conditioner
This cold is more than closed curtains will admit.
We say to ourselves, if not makes these and other means rank
For planned on scheme invented machine cordless reach
Like somewhere sweeping the rooms clean a vacuum robot way,
How could we much admire inventions today,
Here chrome on some machine does number lines
To dot and digit with just solar shines?
It does them, true, no wired on cord enters wall.
Now, we don't think their scheme has done all,
Those men who made the video sound.
But what will folk they list to name their next scheme found?
Such makes and models we behold each year how
Will pave the way for what will follow.
Today, they launching men in spaceships to the moon.
Next, they reside on the rock planet, soon.

Expressive Along Trend

A scene along the realm it bears extreming,
With plenty along where it glamorizing dew misty hem
Perennials at neb toots in flora richness,
The role we love where tinted hues none amiss.
And role a sly hum into, better view, the while
The breeze blowing refinement into heat allowed.
If, now, I settle, I settle on rich.
And trend in how view the role reversing, transmutes
off crowning cluster brims we love, bright shoots.
These poor hems of less and more changing as bird chatter
Awards the flops and rise like acts mediocre.
This coastal edge alters a dewdrop summer hemstitch.
If, now, I settle settlement loves whichever,
I settle for less poor or rich or mediocre.

It's a Style Medium Too Much

Big hips enlarge thighs
of chest large is not large.
It more or less for smaller do,
though more this jolly pitch on the label
song tagged for trendy do.
Some guitar junket of a shirtwaist fad
gets not her thanks for how hang
it hangs in trendy seam.
She pouting slips it pitiful mismatch
of comes off to miss esteem.
A jamboree big is too for jumble.
Why did they make the sheens
a thing-a-majig too big.

Too Large, Too Small

Some store garbs clad with too large, too small.
I fared to look one day for new coat
of a size I could not own to quote.
X-large was too large and large too small.
Medium sleeve would not fit was tight
when I was wearing arms coat though old, fit right.
Why do they change the sizes· too large, too small?

Decade Questions with Trendy or Not

Decade for many the answer wills us
this many questions that years ago much
without answer even if asked.
Like what is tempered glass.
What are laser beam rays,
why do folk live longer today,
how does osmosis process rank.
It ranks for all that living.
Why the hip type pants trendy
and caps and sneakers multi-hue cast.
Is the sun thick solid or just gas.
Will man discover next how leave, bear
what another planet design in lieu
of stay all out stuck with earth polluted.
Depends on science uncovers impending find.
What do rings on trees tell us.
How do Super Jets keep passengers safe behind
some duty weird coincidence attacking with.
What's good about Supersonic Ozone trips.
When did tall boot styles become "it."
Could a fish build a nest deep down in blue sea.
Do people ingest snake meat.
Could a tree grow mixed fruit to eat.
Yes, to all three.
What are Pulsars, what does animal innuendo say,
did a male give birth, how are fossils dated,
all must wait
till what next ranks with write this way.

Designing Buy or Not

If I fancy buying the amber loud car
it's because vivid yellow, carmine red,
tangerine orange and loud blue styles faming cars
seen on streets like never before.

If I think I'll buy the faux fur coat
or the leather slick hazelnut design
or the green suede design jacket
it's because svelt threads I think I'll most buy
need test how hangs before buying.

If I say I'll buy the cell phone, I pad,
3 D machine, computer, anything wireless,
if harm they of radiation case, most likely
these I would hestitate to buy.

If I buy and take standing in supermarket line
instead of take what rates the automatic checker prints
it's because if one flips out odd number days,
I won't think to use it.
Besides, it does take checker jobs away.

Buying This or That

If I go to buy the gold trendy sets locket
and come home driving brighter tinted magenta blue
Porsche instead,
it's because, Gee, I switched mindset, you see,
from gold locket to car hood blue red.
And like anybody, at times I, too, like
loud swanky brazen tinted things.

If I meant to buy the silver culture watch
and back home wearing jazzy reddish gold
culture rank loop earrings instead,
it's because, Wow, long swinging embellishment piece
now hangs bigger the gaudy sheen loops back in style.

If I look to buy chichi fanciful panty hose
and back home with multiple color pink roseate
long cotton stockings instead,
it's because, Ah, cotton weave layer gets thread warm quick
with any blanket season cover had.
And cotton socks rank high for less quick
to slit the rip than panty hose.

Trend With Food

Can you fancy paying $9.00 a load
for loaded peanut butter sandwich?
Not so decade ago. In my day
you made your own peanut butter sandwich
and smacked sloppy lips after you ate.
Now, the novel fig and rosewater jam, good taste,
costs more than Starbuck coffee today
sells for 3 dollars or more a cup.
Organic chicken, cactus tops, cage free eggs,
different organic anything ranks. The food
prices different high for some pockets and goods.
Ocean salmon, octopus, lobster, sushi trendy rank
like $6 hamburgers, dollars mocha ice cream,
frozen yogurt 50¢ an ounce looks to go up.
Too many the price label today for goes up,
I take the second look, second thought whatever.
Pay the different price if choosing whatever,
or settle it, go home different, feeling blue.
But enjoy nut butter sandwich I then eat
gooey stuff gets all stuck to my teeth.

Then to Home I Come

I shall be home late to resides a town there
Sly bats hide and class hummingbirds glide
At regal most city is where in warm air.
Folk call it gold illumines gleaming townside.
I blink at arch cactus the guarded shelf has
How rimming circumference like honors hung
For lovers of dome needles will amass.
Hence, I link rhyming to no scarce done song.
This trek at valley ambience shines my way
To reap the queen of red herbs and spice drink one.
Like fiesta spice fixed leap to cheer I say,
I shall not venture home till once I am done.

Tell my love fair to hear to my quote.
I shall be home late with drink and song note.

Observation

Good ole days. Were they even that?
We like assuming so. What trends in style then?
I can recall some duty mothers would
flip flapjacks on stove's weird circle grate.
You see, it was big pot belly's trendy wood burner,
four rosy hot metal plates for cook on.
Can you envision teenager go,
"When was that mom, in the 50's?
I never knew you for that old."
A tall rude insolence ice box style
would of a sudden drip water on kitchen floor.
Style washing machine designing wide out
squeezed pinky finger off if caught
in roller wringer top designed no pity.
The Good Ole Days? Not if you like indoor toilets,
bathing in bathtub and red licorice sticks.

I also saw some garbs designed odd back then.
But nobody wore trendy hairdo pink
like rose petals or green like watermelon rinds.
Few kids wore bent on cheat exams then,
and, Oh, have parents back behind.
Nil the rap artist trends catalogued
in furthermore raps great or not.
Can you see liprapping pledging,
"These rationale days I own true knowledge
to get me into the academic college."
I really, I do not think so.

So lets assign to black American custom bent;
when blacks were freed from slave days not good;
arranging chorus vents here~
0 hallelujah, 0 hallelujah 0 hallelujah.
God don freed this slave.
There can be no turning back, no turning back,
no turning back for Ole slave ways.

To President Promises

Our President to win, he trumped over others.
He announced pledges for paving roads, cementing
bridges and streets,
adding more jobs, installing thick wall to keep out
Mexico immigrants. And stalwart vows, too, in other warranted
duties abound.
Presidents known f or have a claim in pledge address
regretfully won't suddenly come to pass. ·
African American President before him, the only President
black we ever had.
He laid terrorist leader to rest, instituted insurance!
Abama Care.
He was all for raising incomes and for women's rights heard
vented care.
Weeping with urgency in his voice, he spoke for certain
firearms cease.
He immediately made social marijuana not illegal.
No, he, too, did not every early announced pledge keep.
But was on the right track this world is dutiful about
designing changes.
Yes, I'm a Democrat.

I Cherish Love

I walk to know a pleasing vision rhyme
How glistens the route like shafts from above.
I prize the shelf in trees like jades in rhinestone.
But this most of all, I cherish love.
So few relations from here city so fair
Like few more waves engendered more they rest.
So well I see the silvery evening where
I gaze how bright, still, the avenue east and west.
But this most of all else, I cherish love.
The shadows veiling climb the hill they of
Till I no longer learn what hills uncover.
I see the gloom that starry eyes commenced of,
And know then, if not all love hails from above.
And this most of all, I cherish love.

Customary Supermarket

This go by way supermarket,
it stocks along average we buy average eats
in stock of greens, grains, customary meat etcetera
along customary too the added treats.
It ranks inflation high peculiar
with love abounds in particular.
Since each and every year population steeps up.
Lady who dropped her glass amount spilled
nodded to man around smiled her moan became still
where juice in luscious flavors amount fruit.
Now, all this ranks for starts in something more.
Since price amounts get all the worth,
the start in clip coupons never hurt.

Another Day with Supermarket

Along the brims in supermarket,
appeasement by the palate treats and stacked
can labels, be times it happens,
Our deed in the aisle where starts in lane
Allowed we met as I inspected her form
Facing me, here, meant short and protean
of skin has wrinkles and crow's-feet.
Who helping her there someone reached brand she wanted.
Along with age comes chief status quo;
Growing old is true call some will address.

Enters Mr. Pounds

There comes the trend for style me nets
no ruse my genuine diet
with fruit, grains and vegetables,
and skips the grade of meat adds again, yet
Mr. Pounds loads my girth again.

No matter how agile my exercise
with small weights, stretch bands and walks
and with dance rhythm I have a ball,
Mr. Pounds styles with madly pad thighs.

He's known to give one a present
of bumps and bulges he cannot measure.
There should be more to eat no worry
it will make you too bump curvy.

What shall I do. A fast without food?
If happens, I will pout and brood.

Her Custom Dark Hours She in Residence

Since absolute accord in deep,
Since timid margin sails and midget wax dolls
The average inside the meek wood chest is bin
Benear the little appetites gone to sleep,
It's then she rates the slouch chair appraised fine
For she could likely read a book.
Since home assigning serious regular fare,
It times for little more her tasks afford
Than aptness custom sinks toes
Where shower curtain fits a tub for.
And just before the leisure had here,
Before the soothing turns cold.

A Customary Time Life Generated

It creeps upon who likely of the night designs dark
will creep upon her pouch will bulging quotes
of pain and ecstasy.
And trend would star around pouch sharpens intensifying
pain where Mother Nature.
Then, in the silence night where interludes enter
abode is quieter still and waits the stage
won't play till finally keyed like piano wild verves
would play her other serve
amounts for glee and curiosity.
Then knock the pan, steep the kettle.
Raise the little bootstraps of serving homely cradle
with weeps the wee serves of who of cries
resemble "Why, Why was I born?"

Two for the Wealth

Since this about two, first, for this human,
Human wealth, human deals, he burdened on money.
Else he envisioned best gems trendy had over few.
Add to that chrome of helm's yacht had luxury
It comes along with one the rich man human.
He had this, too, guarded enterprise of gets debt.

The poor man, true, his poor man guard
In had his car plus even debts he had those too
Get the sheen, get the custom style watch he harbored
But less he affords each, all things he harbored.
I squawked sometimes, too, against being poor
Depicts bad worst gets cause for next abandoned.
Needs average, I underline craved sums before
Like essential I may for house and yard blooms plush.
And try as I might to not know what rich is for,
Lo and behold, I'm human in my pitch
Some poor do prosper along beside the rich.

This Age Revolving Trend

Refresh me back remembered folklore,
Said never too old to wonder,
Revolves me back remembered back of yore.

I dreamed, reminds me glad I once
I walked in youth the crowning plumes anon
Enthrall me active do what youth wants.

I wake to rhyming as a strand grooms in,
Revolving model of becomes me here
This aging hoaries hair rearranging.

Aspirant goal for storm I'm half again free,
Decade revolves I'm half again for wealth so near
Amid who ranks the storm in me.

Life takes you up in alteration.
One day, this feeling youthful edge you win.
And how amass a truth here to call,
We age this way if white or brown we in.

They Special This Way

Brown is especial this fair and fine.
Brown as the maple tree branch is fine.
The same this brown depiction dreads us less to say,
"This is the maple grown remarkable this way."
Such tan on looks compliment have to do
With cheek is fair on brown skins hue.
And since it settled in on who man and woman,
It e'er this need fair skin on tan.
Honey gold brown and jetty buffed wine,
Brown is especial this fair and fine.

Tighten Up

This fit you get into,
You tie up into a ball.
Tighten Up
And comes behind slack you set loose
before it tight all.

Inventions Etcetera

Inventions into decades fame, here, a few.
Hufnagel invented artificial heart valve,
U.S. military invented neutron bomb,
Narinder designed fiber-optics.
Robotics, electric wheels, cyberspace losing no caste.
One Daniel Hill for black man surgeon
First man to first perform open-heart surgery.
It was a black man, too, invented traffic lights.
Machine and professionals designed today's go shuttles
Convey of humans and else to go far out in outerspace.
Of sudden this infusion, the line grows dim.
And who invented television, vcr, microwave,
Stethoscope, contact lens ...
Of sudden, I forget.

This Little Poem I Love

Today, in ditch rhetoric
Is sown to here I rest,
I write no chore I hate write over
Denoting sort out waste from line excess.
Where draping words over chair,
I sweep high tales to closet gear
Around rest of the fable toes propped in air.
I won't style if length of line you fear
When import calls, 'Out of time'
Nor make hands verging on rip and tear
The paper if over much rhymes the line.
This is a poem so short of set,
It won't have room for crowd love.
It won't have filth, won't have rhetoric
Nor fix you chained like mutt on glove.

Which people crossed the Delaware
Before you and I adult we'd know?
What are blue oysters, who are fried eels?
What Peking knows, who'd salt, who cares?
Why do I, here, write and small appeal
To rhetoric large of show?
Because great the wee sets
I love to write, even, more.

There Is No Doubt The Poet's Show

There is no doubt the poet's show
What fixed recall polluted with pride
Or flows a moon our troubles deride
To all delay a work to grow.

There is no doubt the poet's show
That walks beside the weeping teardrops
Or runs awhile with wipe the wet clear
That arrives, next, after tears to flow.

Our poet hands do open the stroke
That puts recall to acts turbulent men
Or sits awhile among buds azalea blend
Where minds of image wills spoke.

And what in bare recall put for cause,
Was meant defines the gloom we live a while
Or counts the lovers right along poetic way styling
What cast in hearts was meant will show
What lost awhile should make the assent,
The same we meet as often it went.

Profiling Trends With How She Is

The body indeed has form trendy
How built for goes with vary this trend
Her charm creates infuse the way.
In the house decks with yields and tray,
She'll not rest first, till trendy these
Shops with infrastructure less public overflow
When sleeping wee juveniles tucked firm from cold.
Tight the padlocks where put at night she folds
Her strength conserves for perimeter outdoors.
Civic hill gets full from horde she pours.
A horde of all the knack sources among city when
Her blueprint special for knack odds losing trendy.
From edge to rim rates even each summer she makes
Rich fields clothed while sad earth aches.
Love of Grace and Scorn won't all cease
From where townfolk vary their demeanor.
You know her built between vastly broad this nation.
I know her trendy spring flowers for day meets day
Goes further still, for some urges prod.
Therefore, I know the name, Envira Body.

Custom Beside The True Guides

The squeeze, the mass, the march.
And woman's braids appear swinging wags basson
She won't suddenly quiet the wags.
A sound is even harsh or sweet.
Deed Compassion in the winds
The straw winds melting to a ribbonlike sheet
Denotes the shallow rainbow.
And who of signal where crescendo this verve
Affords the transaction,
We, yet, adapt to tweet, wag, and musicals cars boom.
And else is traffic light
Like much the signal switches off and on custom
Dynamic world we hear beside.

Another Trend Tomorrow

This time you take the beaten path,
Traversing makes for tom tom pace
pounds till satisfied with walk will
At times with go still.
A deed walks at fast and slow traffic street
won't keep the world from car and footsteps.
Compared to years from now
when too dim eyes and slow of feet,
I may not venture far by the ecstacy
how added trade, fad or trend
When too sure foot of walk the distance
a violated circumstance my late years
Try or Might can't explain.
Except walk the tom tom pace how it becomes.
At a late age some sidewalks could become changed
to running sidewalk takes you up and down the route chain.

A Day With Perception

For since we active into time with discovery,
Let me resolves in some agreements near to me
Customary finds like out among the stout
However finds trendy have revenues about

We finding pleasure in they mask golden orchids
Especial keep line of shadows into broaden this mark.
For habitude fruits like coins repaying day and night
To wit by the sprints convolute a tree right.

And tenors rank for tweet they pitching highs, they
Keen lows.
What tokens will refer us back we each only knows.
Then fencing foils a sprint the pitch interpolated grand,
They planted reared up straight in bunch flowers grand.

Let Truth Be Told

Grave or good soul, when will the truth be told.
She said he, true, the venomous darkie
But witnessed move too far to all behold
Who really snatched innocence into his car.
Bright gold the imitation style locket
Looked gold but jewelry copper bronze ink tone.
The painting masterpiece was true for stock
Before it signed but by far landlord known.
Townfolk said vote for son more wealth into.
How soon his flaw gets new assembly man.
This age, the blacks won, true, the conquest they due.
But still more for dark people to win again.

I dare not all assign to this and that.
The soul in truth but torn with add the next act.

In This World We Live

When heat was best on summer trolls the land
Beneath the radiance more rendered flame
With sun the land to much avoid chills aim
How then they so endured the weather's hand!
When they who trek with heavyweight burden
At heat nil bakes nor breaks the winter's dart,
Oh, how then they filled knapsack or wielded cart!
For on sad route that homeless him and her.
They roam where frail the panhandler came nigh.
Oh world, this go with pain, it empties me bare.
What best of remedies cure for when we sigh.
Still, not all hoped for lays claim on despair.
Yet, more than hope must spark for light we ply.
And, yet, what wills regret when times we miss care?

Name Calling

Forever Designs--If that were so, I wouldn't need to
buy more shoes.
Alpha and Omega Hair Shop--Where hair ends up looking
better than it started out looking.
Victory Shop--A shop for trendy designer clothes
and imitations.
Victory Street--Where you think you can't lose.
Lake and Riverside Streets--Where lake and motorboats
Somewhere far, down hard cement walk.
Chatsworth Street--Is any ordinary design tar cement
street worth chat about?
Crossover Street--Where you cross over to trendy
wholesale shop.
Smoke Your Cigarette Shop--Not in my house.
Tap Wellness--You tap till you nap.
Quality Service--Service where having quantity dollars
count.
Lucky Hair Parlor Styles--Not if hair style fell apart
after one visit.
Whole Foods Deli--Where grocery type half-foods
don't count.
Fantastic Doughnuts--Dough you buy more of than
you need.
Chocolate Chip Anything--Too much designs fat on waist line
and hips.
Candy Crunch--If you crunch too much you could break
a tooth.
Trendy Shabby-Looks Clothes--It means trends young people
wear today with shag holes.

My Design is to Be

that certain design
spreading the acceptable theme,
provided that the line is decked,
with printed text awarding motive
for a theme I try to be.

And to be that certain service
displays the worthwhile vision
would not, soon, with played out
the reason manifests itself
:for a skill I try to be.

With this rewarding way to be,
I know that with designing of aim,
it won't rate for aim in mind only.

Incident Assessed to Bar Habit

Eccentric knows between especial inn in town
Chic drinks, male bucks, in smoke air no squanderers shave
Buy her the drinks that merrymakes counters have.
Diversion dizzies who young had her habit renown
This trace in booze trend deroutes her from.

She stopped upstairs to rest for it sorrows her here,
"It. brings on sleep like habit none else I abuse."
She knows the risk with Perils of the bar pales merrymakes
juice.
For bed stains non-descript next her Embarrassment here.
Though much in Shame disowns if gang-banging her fear.

Still, to court she Approbates sueing each one,
The 4 bucks annul admit to rape they wrangle court jests
through,
"She wore her cheap thrills like she given in to."
But judge for silencing male bucks, he aftermaths add on
Scorn knows Blame, since how song and dance number
She still cries to agree with, 'Under twenty one.'

Customarily Before He goes to Sleep

he counts sheep,
or he steals poke along appease
his gentleman steps for simple transacts town.
Except the old Town Hall is torn down
and sports arena off stay the same
at night a slips he in and out.
As nice as meant for swoon the amount,
he less for which electric motives will
or won't dephase trendy little bleats
of one, two, furry little sheep.

Habits Paradigms Between

A mother gives birth
A brick layer lays red brick
A bird builds the nest.
I have no venoms here characterizes
Sweeping slate wiped stark bare since mighty with
resolve
Spirits habits make light of idle chatter.
And folk may even have it different whose girth
Planking boards on purlin eaves. Or be they idleness
wilful scout
seeks finding some new release. And rest is balanced
around midget tremors
Like changing into a city misting ledge where be
someone gravitated;
Lonely for mate his now, loss
Happy for feline lost but found
with neighbor who on the block.
Emotions newly vandalized love when times own relief
Tandem like other sounds amount whistle a cool
sphere.
I hear spring eager on projections in arrears;
Abrupt push cast robin from her nest.

Nocturnal Jamboree Custom

That night she lay at orotund door,
Oh, nocturnal jamboree!
That night she lay where summer given vent
Too glad the summer fee.
Gay sounds were out and nearby unrest
As quilt she on had marble floor fee.

No will she'd list when berries pitted ripe,
Misery heard the owl goad
Had short tu hoots to vague clustered stars.
So glad the birds had night ode.
Glad on worsted trees. All to her discontent how choral
To an old forgotten toad

Too far vanished removed from far stool
As she from Morpheus sick.
"Clacks, too," she said. "And I have, too, heard
How, late in sounding crickets
Inferior clicks loud tattle tales add up
To weird than every break

In every peep came sounds whistling up
In how bird sounds I've known"
Her husband touched with rhyme in his voice
Her sleep came, slowly, drifts down.
I doubt, though the poet kind in him,
If wife, yet, loves that squeak town.

Loves a Grandmother Missing

To her if give one each the hug,
her warm embrace returns them cordial snug
how she left her grandchildren.
Now, home alone where clothes where they land
ranked for love sleep than hunt milestones won't keep:
The trade renounced of stock liquor for barkeep
The public showcase old relic blank at corner mall
Land of Seuss not as tall.
Yard of once thrilled play they romped sports on
old stomping ground is gone
from aged infrastructure new models own front.
And sense forgets for tramp the mall will or won't.
The parlor, the seamstress, bus fare none the same,
not even go to shop inexpensive tags the same.
And comb your hair you brush or miss if unwilling.
Or else give thanks for love of grandchildren.

Refers to Habit Neighbor Loved

This fresh, blunt, even miser
raw curse behind
he blasts two policemen rank
he swearing off since nosed around front porch.
Spunky, though some resemblance spunky less,
his wheelchair he drove next drives behind curse damn
in answer authenticates 'damn' he loves.
Imput in lost his leg,
I never put since knew him not enough to ask how.
But hails were mine betimes, too, I intimated
Could use a trendy going seat pilots push button,
my speech at door jam he for smiling words and fresh
like those he rendered publicly he had sly verb.
Neighbor behind the verbs 'cross court apartment complex
this he even watched me averages, times safely to insides.
Then, happens leased to some occurring found a man
dead, he was dead of heart attack, day in his room.
It rather subleased to sad hearth,
"Parting is such sweet sorrow"
for neighbor departs to.
If one should even ask, the indicative time not docked
of day he suddenly numbs the word;
refers to calm release habit curse now of.
Today, reviving like the wake, again,
I stand, here, twixt how happy and sad.

Which Route to Travel

Zone, if one makes the travel right,
which road?
The Kingshighway gold will rock refining custom
too, burdens load.

Or this enticement as the Broadway style
lights fame,
too, is refining mystifies pilgrim
who trips for lane, lane is
too spell blinding for shake who gifted off drill
whose tasks fall blame
to weary workload.
And strategy renowns rightly faming a verve drill.
And how they else who with assignment
refining highway, they rank for losing
the gold rock task.
Hands off Peace washes clean the milky white ground
to bit excess.
But pilgrim don't brag, don't boast dictate.
Pilgrim on tomorrow another test.

Union Entitles Trend

Immune to worse prescription how union
Prescribes for some institutes have yielded, given in,
To shape a desk advantage won how skill a task medicine.
Tho, here, some wise allotments building franchise
Skills popular license how vested interest
Ingredients credit these coming to:
Mix kind with channeled in diction,
Fuse overflow bills with dun defusing,
Heavy palates take reducing.
Trendy palate lines we amend
Or give in to take the goods with the gains.

Expressive of a Tippler

One beyond repair gone
One near gone
A sad street zone.

He limits thought he blames slack bridle.
And ease it ran for gulping down behind two
Indifferent drafts his counter swigs debunked resolve,
How over two down shot glasses not much booze.

No innocent bystander stands him now.
Inebriate who drove no first trend in disorder,
Gone sad behind he cannot help her somehow
This wee of little girl who cries from loss of mother.

At mainly night trolls motorists, abrupt sot staggers
At autumn the highway members with badges who
Affirm head-on crash mangled who dead cannot rejoice.
And struck meant thrown into coma another came through,

Accusing sot gone wild intruded highway wrong.
Two or 3 drinks or even 5 unbridled forwards how wage
Achieved with school behind swill driver,
"Drink and drive void of sage."

Symmetry Styles

She dwells with a custom habit with vastly built
surroundings in cement bank vast the style.
Symmetry runs in symmetry batch styles
the yards amount to same runs, a sort customary
she lives beside what awarding display tall and short all
between long rows fit under a skyline styling
same banister
hangs over stooped stucco roofs electric wires
fit behind.
Her thin for slender build where people randomly astir,
age in seventy, the same I met at seat stall firmly
how built on western coast, here bus seat familiar same
as city mart.
"How are you, dear; This swelter sweats hot day" she said
the same day.
A next trivia worded uncommon, since, here, you wonder
what phrased without doubt just the same you somehow
doubted.
Still, yet, she said as quite frankly extreming,
"I'm too far spent. I don't have nil to worry about."

Designs on Adam and Eve

Perhaps Adam and Eve would have been known for
style piece also design clad
the void with fig leaf makeshift
beside piece wrap known for temporary fad.
If loin leaves rate fads and I were them,
I might designed stiff leaf the shrine
would pass me shelter from Eden snake
slithering his profile studded with bane brine.
Then, what Peace settled in might life so be,
it ever just the peaceful stamp on time.

Fight The Unrelenting Trap

Gladys took the route to mainly eat
however fat would pad her lap.
To gorge on food prolonged the trap
she fixed no track in its defeat.

John stayed the route with pitfall mugs
he drank himself to trancelike stupor.
No zeal for starts he once stepped for,
his duties lately he would just shrug.
Like odds his younger brother would lug.

What ranks with tracking no ending
for what could be released from no end?

Overseen at Farmstead

Overshadowed of morning mist
in bronze lamp and drafts blowing
downwind to cow grazing
dines on greens he craves,
A deigning refreshes attitudes at summer
depicting interludes.
In huddles of yellow corn of silts, rests.
For these colossal days and mellow nights,
a drifter deigning nods his uneven breathing
where for lack of a better habitat
he longs for, he knows why
he yearns for better dreaming
dreams of him in mind.

Cecil

Of Christabel, this trace at summer prods could sigh;
Of Ophelia, could withhold the fruit and die;
Of Cecil, there's a far tenet song we agree--
Allot my summer blossoms while, yet, I see.

Liquid Sounds

Most like the rolling image sounds
of rich and hardy tide of a seaway,
by even folk lair a poet muse deems announcing
Trump song with what next adjusting sway.

These tinted waves the bright sea I view,
at times I walk beside with a one sided earlobe.
Although another song looking to be due
for the raw gins of another cause I hear

to net my venture cup or sigh.
Profoundly so, it ranks with swoon the pitch
to so profuse the slip like water so awry
that a slip suddenly with changing it to vent

of greatness like gentle waters adore
refreshing tilt. The song to forward moves.
So triumphs victory. Then, will poets more
tell of a soothing sound vents.

And likely, who treks where city tree sap
is the poet, yet, seeks a cause to muse.
And what verse in common with verse overlaps
designing how the life comes alive having issues.

Good Looks, Age Regardless

My, my, my did she look good.
Seventy six years old and looking this good!
Some people tongues query to ask,
"How does your appearance keep good looks intact.
Did you get cosmetic surgery done on chin
and cheeks your choice of rank surgeon styled in?"
to which she would answer in reply,
"It's my choice to know. You likely will find out
what good looks do that people glad about.
Just listen to commercial cosmetic ads on tv
and scour newspaper, tabloids else you read."
Still, some adult tongues criticize good picks her choice
with vilifying lips no link in decade fashions.
And the more some teenagers' choice duds in gaping holes
and sloppy looks pants worn hanging below
nude waistline, the more they appear fickle
as her styles they laugh at and snicker.
What of anything wrong with:
kelly green side pocket coat
choice bow turban hat
vermillion red tunic
red shoes or even lipstick?
She knows her freedom to wear whatever and colors.
She won't be hooking up with someone for
add more babies to mass population explosion.
With few more years to pursue,
she rates for wear what trends and live as wanting to.

Mature About Profile

His jacket resting firm defines firmly
is how he placed it padded on the house
he firmly draped a worn cloak rents along the brown chair.
So silly, trying to all bargain with
these lines tail the scalp down to even marking over arms.
And lines have added even some for trench deep folds
designing jowl cheeks pad the rents dig deep.
A slow acquired identity he admits bulges form
he cannot for all this underwrite nor cheat himself of.
Each year with pouch eyes padded wise, they even more so
than early fabric he from. And what loves he won't keep
he dumps odds in a bag he would like to, but can't own
of some bygones he's yet discerning of what past bygones _
he cannot keep.
This is no facade he faced with everyday
of these 60 approach to seventy.
When passion of a fashion she tramps carpet rooms between,
he likes to think of her love, must it liken him
to screwdriver is like his youngish man gone slow.

Sage and Witty Comments

Trendy white socks turn to fade too fast.
Trend with nylons is they run too fast.
Buy a new suit when old one becomes that old or
shows the hole.
Sell old clothes or donate whether you want to or not.
Too many shoes a trend that clutters up the bit tiny
closet.

To be sure of having money, do the work.
If everybody had money enough. nobody would go hungry
or be homeless.
Anybody with enough talent should be in sync with
enough income.
Some people adjust well to national changes.
Since monetary trend for people with income why is it
Not everybody has one.
People still believe true love what expected
even after it turned tail and ran.

If you think your man of a fashion that's always late
is not out alone you are probably right.

If she didn't really care, she wouldn't more tolerate
his embarrassing ridicules.

If a woman trends in fancy outfits, count on her
spending every dollar she can get on them.

If mate mine trends in fashion clothes like never before,
I'll suspect him of dressing for someone not me.

Only the rich don't have to worry about having trendy
clothes to dress up in for someone.

What average woman who can sew is a good seamstress?
One who fashions clothes won't look homemade.

This mate's husband says she's lazy. But every Italian
entree he cooks, she immediately eats it like crazy.

In Close

This mood in me I'm seen of dingy blood
To wit I'm sown to wit my tannish bud.
A dark perspective however is perceived
Shall dust, here, lot with tone achieved.
Where, near, I'm link with psalmist scene
At felt designing words made keen.
Since oft as spring such words I do book
As dust petunia of how be I am shook.
Abiding what is, none, without man unaided,
Ruin minds the bones when deeply I am shook
About buried set, now, limp they're detained
Who gave life blood for dark all go freely about,
If only, so, to aid what good for man prevails.
For, now, to be, shall tan make sad the lot.

Trend in Competition

This age we love to win at contest,
We look to beat inflated climbs;
And can't stop who dumps the babe put like
Discarded love was left on someone' s doorstep.

Awareness Along The Route

It feels foreboding nights I take
to trace benear coast for public sake.
And realm for how it looks between trace, then, and yet_
Except few more the trailing lights dim on route protect.
The world is like benear jungle it veils allot fees.
Be, then, I can't see for how forest
for the trees.

Centenarians About Friendship

Centenarians still alive
have friends yet arrive
to sit and chat a while
or demonstrate a hot style.
They like when soon inside shops
they relish women in red pops
and salt white hair mops.
They live for years design
to pick their meals fine
and shun friends that only drink wine.

Today's centenarian rife
hears what friends tell of life.
Lucky gals are yet a wife.
Some say tap your toes in bed
wish by tomorrow you're not dead.
Don't sweat about back to school.
Being oldest awards the rule
disinclining be the fool.
They know long friendship's kind tool.

How Soon They Fly

Above me these the flying chariots--
Drives great than the Greeks rode satyrs bare,
Above me astroes swift to the moon.
Their trend to flee must their impending doom.
For man will muse safe place he hath
'Til once he dreads his encompassing wrath.

Be Warned Of Lateness Calls

Raps at my door--Beware the stranger
Behind who voiced in just only three knocks.
At once my paragon fixed him
Eyes stiff doom at quaint holly locks
And weird as icicles carve through dark.
Next day my neighbor had equal mocks
This first discernment, "Last night I called."

Arouse the Sleep Alive to Western Custom

Remakes in how I still my voice inside
remind me how I was, then, my shock stood still.
A sad impeded general night for dreaming turned real
the piece here, the drainboard schism strikes there.
They more than just the crippled tin cans loss of tinsel
allowable so to western earth shakes.

Gone One Little Lad's Love

Little lad swept with grave ill's duty,
Graveside eyes have cried over grave in view.
Why did it have to be you?

He was the only one, son for ply his craft
He loved to plot for toy trends to have.

Little lad gone too soon
Do you will the goldfinch pipe a tune?
Will the little boat float like white swans?
By the hill at trendy garbed how trendy denims once,
You don't, now, laugh or sport despair do.
And whatever else you don't do,
Since I'm perspective,
A wish is for who lives with decade duty select.
Make a difference turning self how meek,
A home oh, so sweet
As little mouths how sweet don't starve;
Live, love living near and far.

Concerning Stranger

In my front middle years I once met
who man of rank garbs for his passion
wore dignified seams of a fashion
the stiff collar like stranger wee threat.

In years older this woman wanted know
who in wine shirt behind her said "hey."
She looked but quick he to say
his laughing "nevermind" though.

In childhood years the girl came close
to who snatched her inside sheen his car.
And fast within local street range.
Oh girls, main, Beware the stranger.
And if you never heard before,
"All that gleams is not gold."

Employing Maxim

One good turn yielded engenders feat deserves another.
Introspection of minds don't count of wee chicks ere
they hatch.
Probing is by a gnome the minute proverbs canon
Shoots the balance how giving strength to even strongholds
hatch
For losing hold on coinage coins phrase
'Cept for few more starts are ornamental here.
'Dumb aspersions pale the song muted,
'Intrepid minds aglow to mimic trendy,
'Late incentives brighten old age.
All good arias came to fair or they amended
Poetry how recited herein.

Responsive of a Female

Demeanor likes a woman
she even so exists with wag equips
her nicer how the jest word quips.

And how she working fire the fare
in full strength is how stormy address
for giving strength to a shield she owns impressive
her diction strikes out gruff acts contrare.

It credits, too, a woman
is not a time machine weaving spells
if kind attempts flop of make gracehood sell.

Who walking splendor down a steep margin
dark words hide till a friend must hear.
She masks the bane if child walks near
she heisting secrets o'er a blear margin.

Demeanor likes a woman
Lovely dues even if sequestered of her,
her shield deflects worse ills from around her.

Trend As In Contemporary

What's in trend the same
May be weaving coif hairstyle
Or mix in camera, tv.
People have addiction
To style of custom woofer track
Behind me not the same.
I traded one music dope in for another
Is nil the same in model track.
Since I don't let it worry me 'in vogue,'
I test this same for what's in trend.

Empty Designs

Come out from empty house of reap
You rhyme so many those notes won't keep.
The time should lot of more than mounds to do
With rhyme and slave model lease runs through.

A Word About Who Smokes

Light rather dark and here a summons
When slightly darkens day beneath for tool douse.
These dull smog days as if sending for up Eden
Declare less taint in sad smog challenges life;
And should allot rain, too, for target lips off smoke
These dim set days when even the mouth smokes.
Word for who yearns this much for choose breath,
Smoking nicotine adds the lungs death.

Directive

I take this route official I am led
Where motive restraints in placid dirt.
There, for when I go; here, for where I am led;
And find this knack with trivia berth
Their ears to numbs which cardinals flirt.

Downhill, I see the tombs paradigm
I have no thought by chance I'll see.
For crusts endow their rank synonym
To red ant cracks and spoil must be
For these are true craters our feet toward flee.

Vestige from the Graves

Here, where the tombs loom high,
A tomb in graves don't sigh
Benear the frilly wreathes and manners nigh.
And member of the hour, this little flower due
Is all I bring to you.

What Achieving Glory Meant

It took abolitionist, a civil war.
It meant speeches, boycotts, sit-ins, marches, beatings,
death to people including martyrs the Martin Luther King Jr.
and Malcom X, all culminating in laws like the Civil Rights
Law enacted.
Between then, there was much our obedience conceded to
because narrow the other choices.
Because we were this obedient, our blacks cleaned the rich
masters plantation house.
Black men and women tilled the fields growing crops.
Because they were obedient, black women gave suck to the master's
young babes and tolerated severe rape.
Because they were obedient, few would even dare learning
to read and write.
Because the race obedient, we endured we drank from separate
water fountains, used separate bathrooms, separate restaurants,
separate hotels and lived in separate neighborhoods.
You said we could not have better paying jobs, better homes,
better education, better areas to live.
We proved you wrong.
You said our mental faculties not equipped for be a scientist,
historian, or surgeon.
We proved you wrong.
You said the time not right to fight prejudice back.
We proved you wrong.
You said our brains too small to learn much.

We proved you wrong. Even if small still we learn.
We prove that after all we endured, we learn enough to help what best this country's adjustments achieve.
And that's a better place to be.